Things to Know Before Opening a Restaurant in Abu Dhabi

First published by Kjøller 2023

Table of Contents

Introduction

Welcome to a comprehensive reference book that explores the various concepts, regulations, and requirements that are vital for anyone interested in opening a restaurant in Abu Dhabi. This book provides invaluable insights and crucial knowledge that you need to have before setting out to start your restaurant.

Running a restaurant involves much more than just pouring your heart and soul into your passion for food. From regulatory requirements to essential terminologies, there is a lot to learn before taking the plunge. This book aims to help readers gain a well-rounded understanding of the intricacies involved in setting up and operating a restaurant in Abu Dhabi. Whether you're an aspiring restaurateur or a seasoned veteran in the industry looking to expand your business, this book is an essential read. So, let's delve into the intricacies of opening a restaurant in Abu Dhabi together.

Abu Dhabi Food Control Authority (ADFCA)

The local regulatory body responsible for ensuring that all restaurants comply with health and safety regulations, food handling requirements, and hygiene standards. ADFCA conducts frequent inspections to ensure restaurants in Abu Dhabi operate in compliance with the law.

Accounting

The systematic recording, analysis, and reporting of financial transactions related to the restaurant's operations. In Abu Dhabi, accounting plays a vital role in maintaining accurate records and complying with tax and regulatory requirements.

Advertising

Marketing initiatives designed to increase awareness of a restaurant's presence, menu, and promotions. In Abu Dhabi, advertising can take many forms, including billboards, online advertising, and social media, and is an essential component of any successful restaurant.

Ajman Municipality

The local government authority responsible for issuing trade licenses and permits, including restaurant licenses, to businesses in Ajman, a neighboring emirate of Abu Dhabi. Diners in Abu Dhabi may travel to Ajman to experience a wider variety of restaurants in the area.

Alcohol License

A permit issued by the Abu Dhabi government allowing a restaurant to serve alcoholic beverages within its premises. Obtaining an alcohol license is a strict requirement in Abu Dhabi and failing to comply can result in serious repercussions, including closure of the restaurant and hefty fines.

Ambience

The character, atmosphere, and aesthetic of a restaurant. Creating a comfortable and welcoming ambience is crucial in Abu Dhabi, where diners often seek out elegant or sophisticated settings to dine.

Arabic Coffee

A traditional coffee beverage in the Middle East made using finely ground beans roasted with spices like cardamom and served in small cups. Arabic coffee is frequently served in traditional Arabic restaurants in Abu Dhabi as an after-dinner beverage.

Arabic Cuisine

A type of cuisine native to the Middle East that encompasses a variety of dishes incorporating ingredients like lamb, chicken, rice, and spices like saffron, turmeric, and cumin. In Abu Dhabi, Arabic cuisine is a popular choice as it reflects the local culture and traditions.

Arancini

A popular dish in Italian cuisine consisting of small balls of deep-fried, breaded rice mixed with cheese or other seasonings. Arancini is a popular dish in Abu Dhabi, adding variety to restaurant menus.

Area

The geographical location where a restaurant is situated, with prime locations attracting higher rents and generating more customer traffic. Abu Dhabi has many popular areas for restaurants such as Yas Island, Saadiyat Island, and the Corniche.

Beverages

Refers to the drinks served in a restaurant. In Abu Dhabi, beverages are an important part of the local culture, which includes coffee, tea, and traditional drinks such as Laban and Karak. It is important to consider the preferences of the local population when designing the beverage menu.

Booking System

A computer-based system that allows customers to make reservations at a restaurant. In Abu Dhabi, it is common to use a booking system to manage the flow of customers and avoid long wait times. The booking system should be user-friendly and easy to access for customers.

Branding

Refers to the process of creating a unique identity for a business. This includes designing a logo, choosing the color scheme, creating a tagline, and developing a marketing strategy. Effective branding can help a restaurant stand out in a crowded market and attract customers. In Abu Dhabi, it is important to consider the local culture and customs when developing branding that appeals to the local population.

Broker

A licensed professional who helps in buying, selling or leasing commercial properties. In Abu Dhabi, a broker is required to have a Real Estate Regulatory Agency (RERA) license to operate. Working with a licensed broker can help in finding the ideal location for a restaurant in Abu Dhabi.

Budget

Pertains to the financial plan of a restaurant. It includes estimating the startup costs, operational costs, and projected revenue. Creating a realistic budget is crucial for the success of a restaurant as it helps in managing cash flow, and identifying potential areas for cost-cutting or investment.

Building Regulations

Refers to the set of rules and guidelines that govern the construction, design, and safety of commercial buildings in Abu Dhabi. These regulations are set by Abu Dhabi's Department of Municipal Affairs and Transport (DMAT). It is important to comply with these regulations when designing and constructing a restaurant.

Busboys

Refers to the staff responsible for clearing tables, refilling glasses, and assisting wait staff. In Abu Dhabi, it is important to provide proper training to busboys to maintain the quality of service and ensure customer satisfaction.

Business License

A legal document that allows a business to operate in Abu Dhabi. It is mandatory to obtain a business license before opening a restaurant in the city. This license is issued by the Department of Economic Development (DED) and its validity can range from one to three years depending on the type of business activity. The application process for a business license involves submitting a set of documents such as passport copies, lease agreement, and NOC from the landlord, among others.

Business Location

Refers to the physical location of the restaurant. Choosing the right location is crucial for the success of a restaurant as it affects the foot traffic, accessibility, and visibility. Factors such as zoning regulations, competition, and population density should be taken into consideration when choosing a location in Abu Dhabi.

Business Plan

A comprehensive document that outlines the business goals, strategies, marketing plan, staffing, and financial projections. A well-thought-out business plan is essential to secure funding from investors, lenders, and partners. In Abu Dhabi, it is important to include an analysis of the local market and competition in the business plan.

Capital Investment

The term pertains to the amount of money required to start a new business. In Abu Dhabi, starting a new restaurant can be quite expensive, and operators need to calculate the capital investment required carefully. It is essential to estimate the costs accurately to avoid running out of funds before the business becomes profitable.

Climate

The term pertains to the typical weather patterns and conditions of a particular region. In Abu Dhabi, the climate is hot and dry, and operators need to consider the impact of the climate on their business operations. For instance, outdoor seating areas may not be suitable for the hot summers, and air conditioning is a must-have requirement for indoor areas.

Competition

The term pertains to the rivalry among businesses offering similar products or services. In Abu Dhabi, the competition in the food industry is fierce, with many established businesses already catering to the market. Operators need to be innovative and offer something unique to stand out from the competition.

Consumer Trends

Refers to the current preferences and behaviors of customers when it comes to dining. In Abu Dhabi, the consumer trends are constantly evolving, and operators need to keep up with the latest trends to meet the changing demands of their customers.

Cost of Living

The overall cost of maintaining a particular standard of living in a specific country or region. Abu Dhabi is known to be an expensive city, and the cost of running a restaurant can be quite high. Operators need to consider the cost of rent, utilities, labor, and ingredients when opening a restaurant in Abu Dhabi.

Cuisine

A term that refers to a specific style of preparing food or cooking associated with a particular region or culture. In Abu Dhabi, the cuisine is diverse, including Arabic, Indian, Persian, and international food. It is essential to research the local food culture and understand what customers in the area prefer before opening a restaurant.

Cuisine Diversity

A term that pertains to the variety of different cuisines available in a specific area. Abu Dhabi is a cosmopolitan city, offering a wide range of diverse cuisines from different parts of the world. Operators need to be aware of the different options available and ensure that their restaurant offers something unique and appealing to customers.

Culinary Training

Refers to the educational and training programs designed to provide individuals with the skills and knowledge required to work in the food industry. In Abu Dhabi, there are various culinary training programs available, and operators can benefit from hiring qualified and trained staff to run their restaurant.

Culture

Refers to the way of life, beliefs, customs, and social behaviors of people in a particular society. Understanding the local culture in Abu Dhabi is crucial when it comes to opening a restaurant. Operators need to take into account the customs and traditions of the local community and ensure that their business is respectful and inclusive.

Customer Service

Refers to the level of service provided to customers when they dine at a restaurant. In Abu Dhabi, customer service is considered essential, and the market is highly competitive. Operators need to provide excellent customer service to attract new customers and retain existing ones.

Data Analysis

Restaurant owners must track their sales, customer behavior, and feedback to make informed decisions and improve their offerings. Data analysis can also help owners identify market trends, customer preferences, and areas for improvement. Integrating technology such as POS systems and CRM can simplify data collection and analysis.

Decor and Ambiance

Customers seek not only good food but also a great dining experience that includes good ambiance and a relaxing atmosphere. Restaurant owners must consider the theme, lighting, music, and interior design to create a unique and welcoming ambiance for their customers.

Delivery Services

With the pandemic, customers rely heavily on delivery services for their meals. Restaurant owners must partner with reliable and efficient delivery services to ensure timely delivery of their food. They can also consider creating their delivery fleet to have better control of their services and provide a seamless customer experience.

Dietary Restrictions

Abu Dhabi has a diverse population with different dietary needs and restrictions. Restaurant owners must cater to vegetarian, vegan, halal, and other dietary restrictions to accommodate all customers. It is also essential to be transparent about allergens and nutritional information in their menu.

Digital Presence

In today's digital age, having a digital presence is vital for any business, including restaurants. Restaurant owners must have a website, official social media pages, and online ordering platforms to keep in touch with customers, expand their reach and generate more sales.

Dining Etiquette

Abu Dhabi has a rich cultural heritage, and it is crucial for restaurant owners to be knowledgeable about dining etiquettes in the region. For instance, eating with the right hand, removing footwear in some establishments, and respecting local customs and traditions, among others. Restaurant owners must educate their staff and customers about these etiquettes to provide a culturally sensitive dining experience.

Discounts and Promotions

Offering discounts and promotions can attract more customers and generate more sales. Restaurant owners can offer loyalty programs, happy hour deals, and holiday discounts, among others. It is also essential to promote these deals through various channels to reach a wider audience.

Documentation and Licenses

Restaurant owners, must obtain the necessary documentation and licenses to operate legally in Abu Dhabi. These include food handling, trade licenses, and municipality permits, among others. It is crucial to ensure that all documents are updated and comply with government regulations to avoid legal issues.

Dubai Food Festival

A yearly festival that promotes regional and international cuisine. It features food-related activities such as cooking contests, dining events, and street food markets, among others. Restaurant owners in Abu Dhabi can participate in the festival to showcase their offerings and expand their network.

Dubai Municipality Guidelines

Restaurant owners must follow the guidelines set by the Dubai Municipality to ensure safety, hygiene, and quality standards. These guidelines cover various aspects such as food handling, storage, preparation, and waste management, among others. Owners must be aware of these guidelines, certified food handlers, and regularly inspected by authorities.

F&B License

Refers to the license that permits a restaurant to operate in Abu Dhabi. To obtain an F&B license, the establishment has to adhere to the legal requirements, like fire and safety regulations, food safety compliance, and environmental hygiene practices.

Fat Tax

Refers to a tax imposed on foods with high fat content to encourage healthy eating habits. In Abu Dhabi, the government has implemented a 50% rebate on soft drinks and 100% excise tax on energy drinks and tobacco products, to promote a healthy lifestyle and reduce non-communicable diseases.

Food Cost

Refers to the expenses incurred in purchasing food products and raw materials necessary for preparing meals. Managing food costs is crucial in the restaurant business in Abu Dhabi, as excessive waste and spoilage can negatively impact profitability and sustainability.

Food Culture

Refers to the customs, practices, and traditions related to food in a particular region or community. Understanding the local food culture is essential for any restaurant in Abu Dhabi, and incorporating traditional dishes and flavors can resonate better with customers.

Food Delivery

Refers to the process of delivering food items from the restaurant to the customers' doorstep. In Abu Dhabi, food delivery is a key aspect of the restaurant business, and there are several popular food delivery service providers like Talabat, Deliveroo, and Zomato.

Food Menu Engineering

Refers to the process of strategically designing a menu to impact customers' purchasing decisions and maximize profits. In Abu Dhabi, it is essential to consider price, taste, and cultural preferences while menu engineering to target the local market.

Food Plating

Refers to the art of arranging food on the plate in an appealing and visually aesthetic way. In Abu Dhabi, food plating is as crucial as food taste since it can impact the customer experience, presentation, and thus, their social media postings. Customers are likely to choose and promote restaurants that feature Instagrammable food.

Food Safety

Refers to the measures taken to ensure that the food served to customers is safe for consumption. It includes proper handling, storage, and preparation of food to prevent contamination that may cause foodborne illnesses. In Abu Dhabi, the Food Control Authority regulates and monitors food safety in all establishments.

Franchise

Refers to a business model where an established brand grants permission to someone to operate a business under its name and systems. Franchising can be a great way to enter the restaurant business in Abu Dhabi, as it provides a business model and brand name with an established customer base.

Front of House

Refers to the restaurant's customer-facing area, including the reception desk, dining hall, and serving sections. Maintaining a hospitable and efficient front of house operation is crucial to creating a great customer experience and generating repeat business.

Globalization

With its diverse population, Abu Dhabi provides a unique opportunity for restaurants to offer global dishes, catering to different nationalities and palates. Understanding and incorporating global cuisine into the menu can help attract customers from various backgrounds and cultures, boosting the restaurant's popularity and revenue.

Gourmet Cuisine

High-quality, exquisite, and often expensive dishes that require exceptional culinary skills, premium ingredients, and meticulous presentation. Abu Dhabi, being a cosmopolitan city, attracts foodies and connoisseurs with various tastes and preferences. Therefore, offering gourmet cuisine can be an advantage for restaurants looking to stand out among the competition and cater to a niche market.

Gourmet Food Festivals

Abu Dhabi hosts several culinary events and food festivals throughout the year that provide an opportunity for restaurants to showcase their menus and attract customers. Participating in these festivals can help build brand awareness, attract new customers, and increase revenue for a restaurant.

Government Regulations

Laws and regulations set by government authorities that oversee the opening and operation of a restaurant in Abu Dhabi. These regulations include obtaining necessary permits, licenses, and fulfilling regulatory requirements such as food safety and hygiene, building code, zoning laws, and taxes. Failing to abide by these regulations could result in fines, suspension or closure of the restaurant, and, in severe cases, legal action.

Green Practices

Being environmentally conscious and implementing green practices, such as reducing waste, using eco-friendly cleaning products, and sourcing locally grown ingredients can attract customers who prioritize sustainability and ethical restaurants.

Gross Profit Margin

Gross profit margin measures the profitability of a restaurant by calculating the total revenue minus the cost of goods sold (COGS). Understanding and monitoring the gross profit margin can help restaurant owners make informed decisions regarding pricing, menu items, and cost-cutting measures.

Group Dining

It is common for families and groups of friends to dine-out in Abu Dhabi, making group dining a crucial factor for restaurant success. Offering group packages, catering to dietary restrictions, and having spacious seating arrangements can attract larger parties and increase revenue for a restaurant.

Guest Experience

The ambiance, decor, and customer service all contribute to the overall guest experience in a restaurant. These factors, coupled with food quality, can make or break the reputation of a restaurant. It is essential to invest in creating an engaging atmosphere and training staff in customer service to provide guests with a memorable dining experience and return to the restaurant.

Guest Feedback

Customer feedback can be valuable for restaurant owners to understand what their customers like and dislike about their restaurant. It is essential to encourage customers to leave feedback, whether positive or negative, and to take their opinions seriously to improve the restaurant's overall performance.

Guest Loyalty Programs

Guest loyalty programs, such as rewards points, discounts, and promotional offers, can incentivize customers to dine-in or make repeat visits to the restaurant. These programs can promote brand loyalty and increase customer retention, leading to higher revenue for the restaurant.

Halal

Halal certification is a must-have if you want to serve food that conforms to Islamic dietary laws in Abu Dhabi. The process of getting your restaurant certified is straightforward, but it involves following specific rules regarding sourcing, preparation, and storage of food. Halal certification ensures that the meat and other products used in the restaurant are slaughtered, handled, and prepared according to Islamic customs.

Halal Kitchen Design

When it comes to kitchen design, you must follow specific rules and regulations in Abu Dhabi for Halal compliance. This may involve separate storage areas for halal and non-halal products or implementing specific processes for the handling of halal meat. You will need to plan your kitchen layout carefully to ensure that it meets these requirements and is efficient for your staff to work in.

Health and Safety Regulations

Abu Dhabi has strict health and safety regulations that all restaurants must adhere to. This includes a variety of factors, such as cleanliness, food storage, hygiene, and staff training. You must ensure that your restaurant has clear policies in place to meet these regulations, as they are strictly enforced, and you could face significant fines and penalties if you are found to be in breach of them.

Healthy Options

Consumers in Abu Dhabi are increasingly health-conscious and are looking for healthy options when dining out. To cater to this market, you must offer a range of healthy options on your menu. This may include vegetarian and vegan dishes, low-calorie options, and meals made with whole foods. Ensure that your healthy options are appealing and tasty to encourage customers to choose them over less healthy options.

High-quality ingredients

To ensure that your food is delicious and well-received, it is essential to source high-quality ingredients. This means selecting fresh, local produce and sourcing meats from reputable suppliers. Be prepared to pay a premium for these ingredients, as quality cannot be compromised when running a successful restaurant in Abu Dhabi.

Hiring staff

Hiring suitable staff can be challenging, but it is essential to find people who can help you to achieve your goals in Abu Dhabi. You must look for people who have experience in the hospitality industry and who are willing to work hard to provide excellent customer service. Ensure that they have the proper qualifications and work permits to work in Abu Dhabi.

Home Delivery

Offering home delivery services is an excellent way to reach a wider audience in Abu Dhabi. You must select a reliable delivery partner and ensure that your packaging and delivery processes are efficient and appealing to customers. You may need to invest in additional resources, such as delivery vehicles and staff to manage orders, but the benefits can be significant.

Hospitality

Abu Dhabi is known for its excellent hospitality, which means providing a warm and welcoming environment for your guests. This includes greeting customers warmly, ensuring that their dining experience is comfortable and enjoyable, and being attentive to their needs throughout their visit. Hospitality is an essential component of running a successful restaurant in Abu Dhabi, and it can help to build a loyal customer base.

Hospitality Laws

As a restaurant owner in Abu Dhabi, you must be familiar with the laws and regulations governing the hospitality industry. These may include regulations around alcohol service, food safety, licensing, and staffing requirements. Ensure that you stay up-to-date with any changes to these regulations, as failing to comply with them could lead to significant penalties or even closure of your business.

Import restrictions

Abu Dhabi has strict import regulations for food items, particularly for fresh produce and meat, which helps to ensure that only high-quality and safe food items are consumed. Restaurants need to comply with these regulations by sourcing their ingredients from approved suppliers to avoid any legal issues.

Import taxes

Restaurants that import food items and ingredients from abroad are subject to import taxes and duties. These taxes can add significant costs to the restaurant's bottom line, so it's important to factor them in when planning the menu and pricing strategy.

Inflation

Inflation is a factor that can impact the profitability of restaurants in Abu Dhabi. As the cost of living continues to soar, restaurants are likely to face higher costs in areas such as rent, utilities, and labor.

Inspection requirements

All restaurants in Abu Dhabi are subject to regular health and safety inspections conducted by the local government authorities. These inspections focus on areas such as food hygiene, cleanliness, and practices.

Insurance

Proper insurance coverage is essential for any restaurant, including protection against liability claims, property damage, and loss of income due to unforeseen circumstances such as fire or flooding.

Interior design regulations

Restaurants in Abu Dhabi need to ensure that their interior design conforms to local regulations. This includes measures such as adequate ventilation and lighting, and appropriate seating arrangements.

International cuisine trends

International cuisine trends influence the local food scene in Abu Dhabi, and restaurateurs must stay abreast of these trends to remain competitive. The city is home to a diverse population, and offering a variety of cuisines is key to attracting and retaining customers.

International suppliers

Given the limited local supply of food items in Abu Dhabi, many restaurants source their ingredients from international suppliers. This requires careful planning and management to ensure timely delivery of ingredients and adherence to import regulations.

Investment

Opening a restaurant in Abu Dhabi requires a substantial investment, particularly in terms of rent, equipment, and labor. It's crucial to have a solid business plan, financial backing, and a clear understanding of the competitive landscape to make the right investment decisions.

Islamic dietary restrictions

Islamic law prohibits the consumption of pork and alcohol. Restaurants in Abu Dhabi should be mindful of these dietary restrictions and ensure that their menus comply with Islamic law. Additionally, some diners may require halal meat, which has been prepared according to Islamic law, so it's important for restaurants to have such options available on their menu.

Jaber Al Ahmad Cultural Center

The Jaber Al Ahmad Cultural Center is a prominent cultural center in Abu Dhabi that hosts musical performances, theater shows, and art exhibitions. Many restaurants located in the vicinity of the center experience high footfall during events, and it is important for them to prepare their staff and menus to cater to this influx of customers.

Jafza license

A Jafza license is a license issued by the Jebel Ali Free Zone Authority (Jafza) in Abu Dhabi, which allows an entity to operate a business in a designated free zone area. Obtaining a Jafza license is necessary for restaurants that plan to operate in a free zone area in Abu Dhabi. The license comes with certain benefits such as exemption from customs duties, zero tax on corporate income, and no restrictions on repatriation of capital and profits.

Jaggery

Jaggery is an ingredient commonly used in Middle Eastern cuisine, and is a type of unrefined sugar made from cane sugar juice or palm tree sap. Many restaurants in Abu Dhabi use jaggery in desserts and other sweet dishes.

Jallab

Jallab is a traditional drink that is served during Ramadan in Abu Dhabi. It is made from a mixture of grape molasses, rose water, and sugar, and is typically served over ice with pine nuts and raisins. Many restaurants serve Jallab as a refreshing drink during Iftar, the time when Muslims break their fast during Ramadan.

Jasmine tea

Jasmine tea is a popular tea variety in Abu Dhabi, and is typically served in traditional Emirati cafes. It is a green tea infused with jasmine flowers, and is known for its subtle floral aroma and delicate taste. Many restaurants in Abu Dhabi serve jasmine tea as a beverage option.

Jelabi

A popular dessert in Abu Dhabi, Jelabi is a deep-fried, syrup-coated pastry that is typically consumed during Ramadan. It is made by mixing flour with yogurt, sugar, and water and deep-frying the mixture in circular shapes. After frying, the jelabi is dipped in warm syrup made of sugar, water, and rosewater. Many restaurants in Abu Dhabi serve jelabi as a dessert item.

Jet lag

For restaurants that plan on receiving international customers, it is essential to understand the effects of jet lag. Jet lag is a temporary sleep disorder that occurs when one's body adjusts to a new time zone. Symptoms include fatigue, irritability, and difficulty concentrating. It is important for restaurants to take this into account when scheduling meetings or events with international customers.

Juices

Abu Dhabi is known for its fresh and exotic juice blends. Popular juices include pomegranate, lemon-mint, and mango. Many restaurants offer juices that are made from locally-sourced fruits, which adds to their appeal. Restaurants should consider including juices in their menu to cater to the local taste.

Julab

Julab is a popular drink in Abu Dhabi that is made by steeping water and sugar with rose petals and mint. It is typically served in traditional Emirati cafes, and is a popular choice for those looking for a refreshing non-alcoholic beverage option. Many restaurants in Abu Dhabi can offer Julab as a unique and refreshing drink option.

Jumeirah Beach Hotel

The Jumeirah Beach Hotel is a luxury hotel in Abu Dhabi that is known for its scenic location and extensive amenities. Many restaurants located in the Jumeirah Beach Hotel cater to a high-end clientele, and it is important for restaurants to understand the customers' preferences and expectations in this regard.

Key suppliers

Establishing relationships with key suppliers is crucial for any restaurant in Abu Dhabi. This includes finding reliable suppliers for ingredients, equipment, and other necessary items. Building strong relationships with suppliers can help to ensure that you receive high-quality products in a timely manner, and may also enable you to negotiate better prices.

Kitchen equipment

Investing in the right kitchen equipment is a crucial aspect of opening a restaurant in Abu Dhabi. Depending on your menu, you may need specialized equipment such as a tandoor oven for cooking naan bread, or an Arabic coffee pot known as a dallah. You'll also need standard equipment such as refrigerators, ovens, and stoves. Ensure that you purchase high quality equipment that will withstand frequent use and meets local safety standards.

Kitchen layout

The arrangement of a restaurant kitchen can greatly impact the efficiency of your operations. It's important to carefully plan the layout of your kitchen to ensure that staff can move around easily and that equipment is strategically placed. It's also crucial to ensure that proper safety measures are in place, such as installing fire suppression systems and having clearly marked exits.

Kitchen management

Managing a busy restaurant kitchen can be a challenging task. It's important to have strong management skills and the ability to delegate tasks effectively. This includes organizing schedules, prioritizing tasks, and communicating effectively with staff. Additionally, having a clear understanding of your restaurant's financials is essential to effectively managing costs and ensuring profitability.

Kitchen safety

As with any restaurant, safety in the kitchen is paramount. Ensure that all staff are trained in proper food handling and safety procedures, including avoiding cross-contamination, practicing good hygiene, and safely using equipment. Having safety measures in place can also help to prevent accidents, such as slips, trips, and falls.

Know your competition

To succeed in the competitive restaurant industry in Abu Dhabi, it's essential to have a deep understanding of your competitors. This includes identifying their strengths and weaknesses, pricing strategies, and menu offerings. By doing so, you can differentiate yourself and create a unique value proposition that will appeal to customers.

Knowledge of local cuisine

Abu Dhabi is known for its diverse and flavorful cuisine, and it's important to have a strong understanding of local dishes and ingredients. This includes learning about traditional Arabic spices, such as za'atar and sumac, as well as popular dishes like falafel and shawarma. Incorporating local flavors and ingredients into your menu can help your restaurant stand out and appeal to local customers.

Knowledge of local regulations

Before opening a restaurant in Abu Dhabi, it's important to have a clear understanding of local regulations governing food service businesses. This includes obtaining proper licenses and permits, adhering to health and safety regulations, and ensuring that your staff is properly trained. Failing to comply with local regulations can result in steep fines or even the closure of your restaurant.

Kosher

Before opening a restaurant in Abu Dhabi that serves kosher food, it's important to understand the requirements of this type of cuisine. Kosher refers to food that conforms to Jewish dietary laws, which prohibit the consumption of certain types of meat and require that food is prepared and served in certain ways. You'll need to find a reliable kosher certifying agency and ensure that your ingredients and preparation methods are compliant.

KPIs

Key performance indicators (KPIs) are metrics that can help you track the success of your restaurant in Abu Dhabi. This can include tracking sales, customer satisfaction, staff turnover, and more. By monitoring these KPIs, you can identify areas for improvement and make data-driven decisions to improve your bottom line.

Labor Law

Labor Law regulates the rights and obligations of employers and employees in the workplace. It covers issues such as employment contracts, working hours, leave, termination, and compensation. It is essential to comply with these laws, as violations can lead to severe fines and penalties.

Landlord-Tenant Law

Landlord-tenant laws protect the rights and obligations of the landlord and tenant in the leasing of a property. These laws govern the lease agreement, security deposit, rent payment, maintenance, and repair responsibilities. One should seek the help of a legal professional to draft and review the lease agreement before signing it.

Language Barriers

Language barriers may occur when communicating with employees, suppliers, or customers who speak Arabic. It is advisable to have at least one Arabic-speaking staff member who can assist in translation and communication.

Licensing Requirements

Licensing requirements are the legal obligations that food establishments must comply with before starting operations. In Abu Dhabi, the Department of Economic Development governs the licensing process. The business owner needs to obtain approval for food safety, smoke control, staffing, hygiene, and more.

Liquor Licensing

Liquor Licenses are required for restaurants serving alcoholic beverages. The level of alcohol served by a restaurant determines the type of license the establishment requires. Liquor licenses are regulated under Abu Dhabi's Alcohol Control Regulations.

Local Laws and Customs

Local laws and customs in Abu Dhabi differ from other countries. For instance, public displays of affection, loud music, and indecent clothing are frowned upon. Understanding and respecting local customs contributes to the success of the restaurant.

Local Marketing Strategies

Local marketing strategies refer to the techniques used to promote the restaurant within Abu Dhabi. These techniques may include local advertising, social media promotions, and partnering with other local businesses. An effective marketing strategy helps to create brand awareness and attract customers.

Local Suppliers

Local suppliers refer to the vendors who supply raw materials and ingredients to the restaurant. The use of local suppliers is beneficial as it supports the local economy and ensures the freshness of the ingredients. One should conduct research and establish reliable relationships with the local suppliers.

Local Taste Preferences

Local taste preferences denote the kinds of food that are commonly consumed by the people of Abu Dhabi. Age, gender, socioeconomic background, and religion influence taste preferences. Local cuisines that are popular in Abu Dhabi include Emirati, Lebanese, Iranian, and Egyptian. One should conduct thorough research and develop a menu that caters to these preferences.

Location

The location of a restaurant plays a crucial role in its success. One should choose a location with high foot traffic, ample parking space, and accessible transportation. In Abu Dhabi, popular areas for restaurants include Marina Village, Al Bateen, and Corniche.

Management

Effective management is essential for any successful restaurant in Abu Dhabi. This includes hiring and training staff, scheduling employees, managing finances, and ensuring quality control. The management team should have experience in the food and hospitality industry and be able to handle customer complaints and feedback.

Market Research

Before opening a restaurant in Abu Dhabi, it is crucial to conduct thorough market research in order to determine the potential demand for the restaurant, identify the target market, and understand the competition. Market research should include analyzing consumer trends, evaluating the economic landscape, and gathering data on local demographics.

Marketing and Advertising

A strategic marketing and advertising plan is vital to promote a new restaurant, engage with target audiences, and create brand awareness in Abu Dhabi. Marketing efforts should include online and offline channels such as social media, influencer marketing, print ads, and billboards. It is also important to create a compelling brand identity that reflects the restaurant's values and unique selling proposition (USP).

Memorandum of Understanding

A memorandum of understanding (MOU) is a formal agreement between two parties that outlines the terms and conditions of their relationship. In the restaurant industry, MOUs can be used to establish partnerships or collaborations between various entities such as suppliers, distributors, or marketing agencies. MOUs should include information such as the purpose of the agreement, the scope of work, and the roles and responsibilities of each party.

Menu Creation

The process of designing a restaurant menu is an important aspect of opening a successful restaurant in Abu Dhabi. A well-designed menu is essential to engage customers and retain them. The menu should feature a wide selection of dishes that are carefully crafted to appeal to different dietary requirements and preferences, including vegan, gluten-free, and low-carb options. It is also important to include traditional Emirati dishes on the menu to showcase the local cuisine which is an important part of the dining experience in Abu Dhabi. The menu design should be visually appealing, easy to read, and effectively communicate the restaurant's brand and values.

Menu Engineering

Menu engineering is the practice of strategically pricing and positioning menu items to maximize profits and sales. This involves analyzing the popularity and profitability of different dishes, adjusting portion sizes and pricing, and strategically placing items on the menu. Additionally, highlighting high-margin items and add-ons on the menu such as appetizers, desserts, and beverages can also increase revenue.

Mise en Place

Mise en place is a French culinary term that refers to the process of preparing and organizing ingredients and equipment prior to cooking. This involves prepping ingredients, measuring out portions, and setting up the kitchen workspace. Having a well-organized mise en place is essential for efficient kitchen operations and ensuring consistent quality of dishes. It is also important to train kitchen staff on proper mise en place procedures to minimize errors and delays in preparation.

Mood and Atmosphere

The mood and atmosphere of a restaurant play an important role in the overall dining experience for customers in Abu Dhabi. The decor, lighting, music, and seating arrangements should create a warm and welcoming ambiance that reflects the restaurant's brand and values. Additionally, it is important to consider noise levels, ventilation, and temperature control to ensure customer comfort.

Nationalization

Refers to the policy of promoting the interests of the citizens of a particular country, by restricting the ownership, control, or management of industries or businesses in foreign hands. In Abu Dhabi, the government has been gradually promoting nationalization by enacting laws that promote the employment of Emirati Nationals in key positions in the private sector, including the restaurant industry.

Network Planning

Refers to the process of optimizing a restaurant's operations and logistics to reduce costs and increase efficiency. In Abu Dhabi, network planning may involve identifying the most cost-effective supply chains for food and equipment, optimizing staffing levels and work schedules, and using technology to streamline ordering and payment processes.

New Market Development

Refers to the process of identifying and developing new markets for a restaurant's products or services. In Abu Dhabi, new market development may involve targeting tourist hotspots, creating strategic partnerships with hotels or event planners, or collaborating with local influencers to promote a restaurant's offerings.

Niche Market

A small but specific segment of the market that has unique needs, interests, or preferences. Identifying and catering to a niche market can lead to a loyal customer base and higher profit margins for a restaurant. In Abu Dhabi, niche markets may include vegan or vegetarian restaurants, seafood restaurants, or fusion cuisine restaurants.

No Smoking Policy

Abu Dhabi has introduced a strict no-smoking policy, which prohibits smoking in enclosed public spaces, including restaurants, cafes, and fast-food establishments. All restaurants must display "no smoking" signs prominently and enforce the policy by taking appropriate measures against violators.

Noc Certificate

Stands for No Objection Certificate, which is a document issued by the Abu Dhabi Municipality, which confirms that a proposed restaurant or business is permitted to operate in a particular area. It also confirms that a restaurant is compliant with all public health and safety regulations, including waste disposal, maintenance, and hygiene.

Noise Pollution

Refers to excessive or disturbing noise levels that can negatively impact the health and wellbeing of people. In Abu Dhabi, restaurants must ensure that they are compliant with local noise regulations, which limit the decibel levels of music, machinery, and other sources of noise pollution.

Non-Compete Clause

A legal agreement that prohibits an employee or business owner from competing with their former employer or business within a specific geographical area or for a particular period. Restaurant owners in Abu Dhabi may be asked to sign a non-compete clause as part of their employment contract, which ensures that they do not set up a competing business in the same area for a particular period.

Non-Disclosure Agreement

A legal agreement that prohibits an employee, vendor, or other third-party from disclosing confidential information about a restaurant's operations or plans. In Abu Dhabi, restaurant owners may use non-disclosure agreements to protect their trade secrets and prevent competitors from gaining an unfair advantage.

Nutritional Labeling

A requirement by the Abu Dhabi Food Control Authority for restaurants to provide nutritional information on their menu items. The labeling must include the calorie count, fat content, and other nutritional values of each dish. This requirement aims to promote transparency and enable customers to make informed choices about their food.

Patrons

Customers of the restaurant. Abu Dhabi is a cosmopolitan city with a diverse population, so restaurant owners need to cater to locals and tourists alike. Menu offerings, décor, and ambiance should appeal to a wide range of cultures and tastes.

Payment Methods

Offering various payment options such as cash, credit cards, and mobile payments. Abu Dhabi is a technologically advanced city, and many residents prefer digital or contactless payments.

Performance Metrics

Monitoring financial performance and customer satisfaction to make data-driven decisions. Restaurant owners should track revenue, profit margins, customer feedback, and reviews to continually improve their operations.

Permits and Licenses

Required documents needed for opening a restaurant in Abu Dhabi. These include a trade license, a food and beverage license, an alcohol license, a health and safety certificate, and a civil defense certificate. All permits must be obtained prior to the opening of the establishment.

Post-Opening Operations

Management of day-to-day activities such as customer service, food preparation, hygiene, and safety. Staff training and adherence to local laws and regulations are essential.

Presentation

The appearance of dishes is just as important as their taste. Restaurant owners in Abu Dhabi should prioritize attractive presentation and consider cultural preferences (such as halal or vegetarian options).

Pricing Strategy

Determining the cost of menu items to ensure profitability while remaining competitive. The cost of living in Abu Dhabi is relatively high, so pricing should reflect this but not be prohibitively expensive for customers.

Privacy

Ensuring customers' privacy and comfort while dining. Abu Dhabi permits the sale of alcohol but has strict regulations regarding its consumption in public. Restaurant owners should provide private dining areas or partitions to offer a more intimate experience.

Procurement

Sourcing raw materials such as meat, seafood, vegetables, and spices. Restaurant owners should prioritize local suppliers to support the community and reduce costs. Abu Dhabi is known for its fresh produce and seafood, and restaurant owners should take advantage of these options wherever possible.

Promotions

Generating buzz and attracting customers through various marketing techniques. Restaurants in Abu Dhabi should advertise on social media and other platforms, offer loyalty programs and seasonal deals, and partner with local influencers to expand their reach.

Qatar blockade

Refers to the dispute between Qatar and neighboring countries that started in June 2017, resulting in the blockade of Qatar by several countries, including the UAE. This led to restrictions on transportation, trade, and travel, affecting the food supply chain and the hospitality industry in the UAE, including Abu Dhabi.

QR code

Refers to a two-dimensional barcode that can be scanned using a smartphone's camera to access information or make payments. QR codes are becoming increasingly popular in restaurants in Abu Dhabi, as they offer a contactless solution for ordering, paying, and gathering customer feedback.

Quality control

Refers to the process of maintaining the consistency and high standards of food, service, hygiene, and ambiance in a restaurant to meet customer expectations. Effective quality control includes regular inspection of kitchen and dining areas for cleanliness, employee training, menu planning, customer feedback, and continuous improvement of processes.

Quantity discounts

Refers to the discounts offered by suppliers or vendors to restaurants who buy large quantities of products at once. Quantity discounts may be based on the quantity purchased, the frequency of purchases, or a combination of both. Restaurant owners should negotiate with their suppliers to get the best possible deals without compromising on quality.

Quarter rent

Refers to the payment of rent in advance for every quarter (three months) in a commercial lease agreement. In Abu Dhabi, landlords usually ask for a security deposit and quarterly rent payments from tenants, including restaurants, as a guarantee of payment and financial security.

Quesadilla

Refers to a popular Mexican dish made with tortillas filled with cheese, meat, vegetables, and other toppings. Quesadillas can be served as appetizers or entrees in restaurants, including Mexican and Tex-Mex establishments in Abu Dhabi.

Queue management

Refers to the efficient management of customer waiting times in a restaurant, especially during peak hours. This includes offering reservations, optimizing table turnover, providing adequate seating, and ensuring proper communication between the front-of-house and back-of-house staff to minimize wait times and enhance customer experience.

Quick Service Restaurant (QSR)

Refers to a type of restaurant that offers fast food, counter service, and limited dine-in seating. QSRs typically have a simple menu, low prices, and fast service, making them popular for on-the-go customers. Examples include McDonald's, Subway, and KFC.

Quiet evenings

Refers to the days of the week when restaurant business is slower, resulting in lower foot traffic and sales. In Abu Dhabi, quiet evenings may vary depending on factors such as location, type of cuisine, and customer preferences. Restaurant owners should monitor their sales metrics and adjust their staffing and inventory accordingly to optimize profitability.

Quota

Refers to the maximum number of employees allowed to work in a restaurant in Abu Dhabi as per the labor laws. The quota varies depending on the restaurant's size, type, and location. It is essential to check the quota limits before hiring employees to avoid legal issues with the government authorities.

Recruit and Train Employees

- Recruiting and training competent employees is essential. Getting the right staff could help in the success of your restaurant, the staff needs to be good at their job, and they should also have a friendly and welcoming demeanor. Make sure to follow labor law and provide health insurance and food allowances for the employees.

Rent

- Rent is a major consideration when setting up a restaurant in Abu Dhabi. There are four types of lease agreements possible in Abu Dhabi, Commercial lease which applies to restaurants and office space, Retail lease for space in shopping malls, Industrial leases for large warehouse space, and Residential landlord and tenant lease agreements.

Research

- Before opening a restaurant in Abu Dhabi, you need to research about the market, competitor analysis, and their targeted audience. Research is key to know what works, and what doesn't work so that you know what to do, also the research help save time and costs in the long run.

Reservation Systems

- In Abu Dhabi, with the help of the internet, it's become essential for restaurant reservations to adopt technology-driven solutions to manage their bookings, food orders and even sending out promotions. Implementing a reservation system can help increase foot traffic in the restaurant, and it reduces the chances of overbooking, which results in unhappy customers waiting for their tables.

Restaurant Concept

- Determining your restaurant's concept is your chance to refine your menu, branding, and overall ambiance of your restaurant. Any theme is possible to get started on the restaurant concept from street food to fine dining.

Restaurant Design

- Your restaurant interior design is essential in impressing your customers, creating a memorable experience, and ultimately boosting sales. A thoughtful design, both in exterior and interior elements, contributes to customers' satisfaction, and it is what defines your restaurant's ambiance and brand identity.

Restaurant Marketing

- It's essential to have an effective marketing strategy in place as it can have a big impact on the business's bottom line. You can use various marketing strategies, from social media promotions, discount coupons via messaging software like Watermelon.co to newspaper ads, and targeted emails or newsletters.

Revenue

- Revenue is the income generated by a restaurant for a particular period, and calculating restaurant revenue is essential for knowing the financial health of the business. To maximize revenue, it's essential to do a cost-benefit analysis that considers both the cost of operations and the price of the menu items.

Rough Idea of investment

- Opening a restaurant in Abu Dhabi requires a significant financial investment, and you'll need to consider rent, utilities, marketing, employee salaries, equipment, and inventory costs. It is important to have a rough idea of the capital structure so that you can make informed decisions about the business finances ahead.

Rules and Regulations

- Regulations that apply to the food service industry in Abu Dhabi. To start a restaurant in Abu Dhabi, you must follow the rules and regulations set by The Abu Dhabi Municipality. The regulations are very extensive and cover everything from food safety, menu display, design, and hygiene to labor law.

Sales Forecast

Refers to the estimation of the expected revenue and expenses of the restaurant for a certain period. A clear understanding of the sales forecast can help with budgeting, inventory management, and staffing decisions.

Sanitation

Refers to the practice of maintaining cleanliness and hygiene in the restaurant to prevent the spread of diseases and ensure food safety. Compliance with the food safety regulations set by the Abu Dhabi government is vital for the success of the restaurant.

Seating

Refers to the arrangement of tables and chairs in the restaurant. Proper seating arrangements need to be considered to accommodate different group sizes, provide adequate spacing between tables, and ensure easy movement of staff and guests.

Service

Refers to the quality of the dining experience provided to the customers. Excellent service includes attentive and friendly staff, efficient and prompt delivery of food and drinks, and a comfortable and inviting atmosphere.

Signage

Refers to the visible signs and graphics that promote the restaurant and guide guests to the entrance or various areas of the restaurant. Effective signage is important for attracting customers and enhancing their overall dining experience.

Social Media

Refers to the use of social media platforms to promote the restaurant and engage with customers. Establishing an online presence and regularly posting updates can help to increase brand awareness and customer loyalty.

Specials

Refers to the daily or weekly specials offered by the restaurant, which could include seasonal or local ingredients, unique dishes, or discounted prices. Specials can attract new customers and provide regulars with exciting options to try.

Staffing

Refers to the process of finding and hiring qualified and competent employees for various roles in the restaurant such as head chef, sous chef, servers, and bartenders. Proper training and management of employees are also essential for maintaining a positive work environment and delivering excellent customer service.

Style

Refers to the overall aesthetic and atmosphere of the restaurant. The style should be consistent with the cuisine and target demographic of the restaurant and create a memorable and enjoyable dining experience for the guests.

Suppliers

Refers to the companies or individuals who provide goods and materials for the restaurant. It is important to research and establish relationships with reliable suppliers to ensure consistent quality and timely delivery of ingredients and supplies.

Tableware

Every restaurant should invest in high-quality tableware, including plates, glasses, and cutlery. This contributes to the overall ambiance and customer experience and should be chosen based on the target market and restaurant concept.

Talent Acquisition

Employees are the backbone of any restaurant, so it is essential to recruit and train the right team. This involves applicant screening, conducting interviews, and providing effective on-the-job training.

Target Market

Identifying the restaurant's target customer demographic by considering factors such as age, income level, and location, is an important step in establishing a restaurant business. This will help owners tailor their menu, decor, and marketing plan to the intended audience.

Taste Testing

A process of evaluating food quality and consistency, which is important to ensure customer satisfaction. Restaurant owners should sample menu items before opening to confirm their quality, taste, and presentation.

Taxation

Abu Dhabi has various taxes applicable to businesses, such as Corporate Income Tax and Value Added Tax. Understanding the taxation system is crucial for budgeting and compliance purposes.

Technology

Implementing the current technological advances is vital to maintaining a successful restaurant. Some examples include the use of Point of Sale (POS) Systems to monitor sales and inventory management software to track orders and supplies.

Third-Party Delivery Services

With the increase in demand for delivery services, it is essential to partner with reputable third-party delivery services to meet customer needs. Owners should choose delivery partners that have a reliable track record, reasonable pricing, and can handle food safely and securely.

Trade License

A legal document that permits a business to operate in Abu Dhabi. It is issued by the Department of Economic Development and is required for every type of business, including restaurants.

Trademark Registration

Registering a trademark for the restaurant can provide legal protection against potential infringement by other businesses operating in Abu Dhabi. The trademark registration process involves filing applications, paying fees, and following legal procedures.

Training Programs

A structured training program for restaurant staff is essential for providing efficient service and maintaining consistency in food quality, hygiene, and safety standards. These programs can include orientation sessions, workshops, and ongoing training to ensure that all employees are well-trained and informed.

UAE Food Safety Guidelines

The UAE government follows strict food safety guidelines to ensure public safety. As a restaurant owner in Abu Dhabi, you must adhere to these guidelines to obtain a food safety certification. This includes maintaining proper hygiene and cleanliness, sourcing fresh ingredients, and storing food at the right temperature to prevent contamination.

Understanding Local Culture

It is important to familiarize yourself with the local Emirati culture before starting a restaurant in Abu Dhabi. This includes understanding the religious and social norms, etiquette, and customs.

Understanding the Market

Conduct market research to understand the demand and competition in Abu Dhabi's restaurant industry. You need to identify the gaps in the market and cater to specific customer preferences.

Uniform Pricing

Pricing plays a crucial role in the success of your restaurant. You need to maintain uniform pricing to avoid confusion and dissatisfaction among customers. You should also offer discounts and promotions to attract customers.

Uniforms

Your restaurant staff must wear a uniform that complies with the dress code regulations set by the Abu Dhabi government. Uniforms must be clean, well-fitted, and appropriate for the job. It is important to consider the cultural sensitivities when choosing the uniform.

Unique Selling Proposition

To make your restaurant stand out in a highly competitive market, you need to have a unique selling proposition. This could be the quality of your food, the ambience, or the service you offer.

Upfront Costs

Starting a restaurant in Abu Dhabi can be expensive due to the high rents and cost of living. You need to factor in the upfront costs of equipment, licenses, permits, and staff salaries.

Usage Restrictions

As per the UAE law, there are certain restrictions on the usage of certain ingredients such as pork and alcohol. You must ensure that your restaurant complies with these restrictions and communicates them to the customers.

User-Friendly Technology

Adopt user-friendly technology such as online ordering system, digital payments, and restaurant management software to enhance the customer experience and streamline your operations.

Utilities

You must ensure that your restaurant has access to uninterrupted utilities such as electricity, water, and gas. This is important for the smooth operation of your business.

VAT

Value-added tax (VAT) is a tax on goods and services that will apply to all businesses with an annual income of over AED375,000. It is crucial to understand VAT registration and payment requirements to avoid legal and financial penalties.

Vegan and vegetarian options

Providing vegan and vegetarian options is becoming increasingly important as more people adopt meat-free lifestyles. Creating a diverse and delicious menu can attract a wider customer base and increase revenue.

Vendor contracts

Vendor contracts outline mutual expectations and can help avoid misunderstandings and conflicts. Ensure that all contracts are negotiated and reviewed by a legal expert to protect your business interests.

Vendor relations

Building strong relationships with vendors is paramount to a successful restaurant business. It is essential to ensure timely and quality supplies, regular communication, and fair negotiations with vendors.

Ventilation

Proper ventilation is necessary to ensure a safe and enjoyable dining experience. It is essential to comply with all ventilation and air quality regulations to avoid fines and protect customers and staff.

Venue selection

Choosing the right location is vital for a restaurant's success. Consider factors such as foot traffic, accessibility, parking, zoning regulations, and competition when selecting a venue.

VIP services

Offering VIP services can help a restaurant stand out from competitors. It may include private dining rooms, personalized menu options, exclusive events, and unique customer experiences.

Virtual ordering

In response to the COVID-19 pandemic, virtual ordering and delivery services have become crucial for restaurant survival. It is essential to research and invest in reliable and accessible virtual ordering systems to keep up with current trends.

Visa requirements

Requirements for obtaining a visa for Abu Dhabi will depend on the country of origin. It is necessary to ensure that all staff, especially foreign workers, have the proper documentation to work in the UAE.

Waitstaff training

Waitstaff in Abu Dhabi restaurants must be knowledgeable about the cuisine, culture, and customs of the region. They should be able to provide guests with information about dishes, answer questions about ingredients and preparation methods, and offer recommendations based on dietary restrictions or preferences.

Waste management

It is important for restaurants to have a waste management plan in place before opening in Abu Dhabi. The city has strict regulations on the disposal of food waste and other types of garbage, and restaurants must comply with these rules or face fines or penalties. Some restaurants even use composting and recycling systems to reduce their waste and help the environment.

Water regulations

The water regulations for restaurants in Abu Dhabi are quite strict. The water used for drinking, cooking, and washing dishes must meet certain standards that are set by the government. Water must be filtered and treated to remove impurities, and restaurants must regularly test the quality of their water to ensure it is safe for consumption.

Website design

In today's digital age, a restaurant's website is often the first point of contact for potential customers. A well-designed website that is easy to navigate and features professional photography and engaging descriptive text can help restaurants stand out from the competition and attract new customers.

Weekly specials

Offering weekly specials is a great way for restaurants in Abu Dhabi to keep their menus fresh and exciting. Specials can be based on seasonal ingredients, local traditions, or global culinary trends. Restaurants should promote their specials on social media, their website, and through other marketing channels to encourage repeat business.

Western cuisine

While there is a growing interest in global cuisine in Abu Dhabi, there is still a strong demand for traditional Western dishes such as burgers, pizza, and steak. Recognizing and catering to this demand can help restaurants attract a wider range of customers.

Wi-Fi access

Providing reliable and fast Wi-Fi access is essential for restaurants in Abu Dhabi. Many customers expect to be able to use their mobile devices while dining, and offering free Wi-Fi can be a simple yet effective way to enhance the customer experience and encourage repeat business.

Wine lists

Abu Dhabi has strict regulations on the sale and consumption of alcohol, so restaurants must obtain a special license to serve wine and other alcoholic beverages. Restaurants should also be aware of local customs and offer a balanced and diverse wine list that respects cultural and religious traditions.

Women's attire

Women who work in restaurants in Abu Dhabi must dress modestly and cover their shoulders and knees. This is in accordance with local customs and traditions, and failure to comply may result in fines or legal action.

Work visas

Foreign nationals who want to work in Abu Dhabi restaurants must first obtain a work visa from the government. The process can take several weeks or months and requires the submission of various documents and paperwork. Restaurants should be aware of these requirements and allow ample time for the visa process.

Yacht Club

Abu Dhabi is a hub for luxury yacht owners and the yacht club is a popular spot for tourists and residents. Having a restaurant in the yacht club can increase visibility and access to the high-income demographic.

Yas Island

A man-made island in Abu Dhabi that is a major tourist attraction. It is home to several theme parks, luxury hotels, restaurants, and entertainment venues. Having your restaurant located in Yas Island increases visibility and accessibility for tourists.

Yas Mall

One of the largest shopping malls in Abu Dhabi, located on Yas Island. Having your restaurant in Yas Mall can attract customers who are looking for a quick meal while shopping.

Year-Round Business

Abu Dhabi experiences hot weather all year round, which means the demand for indoor restaurants is high. Ensure that your restaurant has adequate air conditioning to cater for customers throughout the year.

Yellow Cuisine

UAE cuisine that is typically mild and fragrant, using herbs like saffron, turmeric, and neem. Incorporating local cuisine into your restaurant menu is essential in attracting customers.

Yellow Zone

A designated area in Abu Dhabi where restaurants are required to have a maximum of 20% seating capacity in order to comply with Covid-19 regulations. It is important to consider the impact of the yellow zone restrictions on your restaurant's seating capacity and operations.

Yield Management

A pricing strategy based on the idea of adjusting prices according to demand. Yield management is especially important in Abu Dhabi's competitive restaurant industry, where pricing can make or break a business.

Yield Per Cover (YPC)

A financial metric used to measure revenue per customers. Maximizing YPC is important for your restaurant's profitability.

Yoga Brunch

A popular brunch trend in Abu Dhabi, where diners participate in a yoga class before enjoying a healthy brunch. Hosting Yoga Brunches in your restaurant can attract a health-conscious demographic.

Yum Cha

A traditional Cantonese brunch, where diners enjoy dim sum and tea. Offering brunch or dim sum menus can cater to residents and tourists who are interested in trying new cuisine.

www.ingramcontent.com/pod-product-compliance
Lightning Source LLC
Chambersburg PA
CBHW071030220526
45467CB00004B/1597